W9-ATB-283

Wild WATER

Canoeing and Kayaking

NEIL CHAMPION

A+

Smart Apple Media

Published by Smart Apple Media, an imprint of Black Rabbit Books
P.O. Box 3263, Mankato, Minnesota 56002
www.blackrabbitbooks.com

U.S. publication copyright © 2013 Smart Apple Media. International
copyright reserved in all countries. No part of this book may be
reproduced in any form without written permission from the publisher.

Printed in the United States of America at Corporate Graphics,
North Mankato, Minnesota

Library of Congress Cataloging-in-Publication Data
Champion, Neil.
  Wild water : canoeing and kayaking / by Neil Champion.
     p. cm. — (Adventure outdoors)
  Includes index.
  Summary: "Describes how to canoe and kayak by exploring the boat
design, gear needed, and paddling techniques used for both water
sports. Explains the 6 white water grades and other risks and teaches
how to handle a capsized boat. Includes labels, diagrams, and
reading quiz"—Provided by publisher.
  ISBN 978-1-59920-812-1 (library binding)
  1. Canoes and canoeing--Juvenile literature. 2. Kayaking—
Juvenile literature. I. Title.
  GV784.3.C54 2013
  797.122--dc23

                          2011047436

Created by Appleseed Editions, Ltd.
Designed and illustrated by Guy Callaby
Edited by Mary-Jane Wilkins
Picture research by Su Alexander

All rights reserved. No part of this publication may be
reproduced, stored in a retrieval system, or transmitted
in any form or by any means, electronic, mechanical,
photocopying, recording or otherwise without prior
permission of the publisher.

Picture credits
l = left, r = right, c = center, t = top, b = bottom
page 1 Jupiterimages/Thinkstock; 2,4,5,6 & 7t Thinkstock, 7b Wikimedia
Commons/Ruth Crafer; 8t Oleg Zabielin/Shutterstock, c Brian Lasenby/
Shutterstock, b Thinkstock; 9 Chudakov/Shutterstock; 10 Jupiterimages/
Thinkstock; 13t Thinkstock, b Wikimedia Commons/P J Blalock; 14
Thomas Northcut/Thinkstock; 15t Thinkstock, b Chudakov/Shutterstock;
17 Lane V Erickson/Shutterstock; 18 David Kay/Shutterstock; 19 Mark
Yuill/Shutterstock, r Comstock/Thinkstock; 20 Falk Kienas/Shutterstock;
21 Thinkstock; 22 Hemera Technologies/Thinkstock; 23 Mike Powell/
Thinkstock; 24 Comstock Images Thinkstock; 25l Klaitu/Shutterstock,
r Thomas Northcut/Thinkstock; 26 Vince Clements/Shutterstock;
27 Hemera Technologies/Thinkstock, r Thinkstock; 28 Thinkstock;
29t Wikimedia Commons/ National Geographic volume 31 1917/
George R King, b Vereshchagin Dmitry/Shutterstock; 31 Marekuliasz/
Shutterstock; 32t Thinkstock, b Jupiterimages/Thinkstock
Cover: Monkey Business Images/Shutterstock

PO1443
2-2012

9 8 7 6 5 4 3 2 1

Contents

Let's Go Paddling! 4

Getting Started 6

Boats and Water 8

Boat Design 10

Danger in the Water! 12

Learning to Kayak 14

Learning to Canoe 16

White Water 18

Emergency on the River! 20

Sea Kayaking 22

Going on a Journey 24

Entering Competitions 26

What do you know about paddling? 28

Glossary 30

Websites and Books 31

Index 32

Let's Go Paddling!

Earth is a very wet place. Its rivers, lakes, and seas provide us with food and ways of moving around, as well as adventure and fun.

The Inuit (the native peoples of the Arctic) were the first to move around on water in small boats called kayaks. Their small, one-person boats navigated the waterways of Canada and Greenland, where ice often blocks the way. The Inuit covered their boats with a tight skin to keep water out—today this is called a **spraydeck**. Other native peoples around the world used open canoes in less extreme conditions. The skills they developed have made canoeing and kayaking popular water sports. Wherever you live, you can enjoy learning to paddle.

A paddler takes on the challenge of riding white water and shoots the rapids in a kayak.

You can safely learn to kayak in a swimming pool.

Rising to the Challenge

Imagine you're in a small boat on a river, nearing some rapids. White water swirls around you, drawing your boat toward rocks and whirlpools. You have to paddle skillfully to avoid them. Then you're shooting along midstream with running water all around. Can you stay in control? What's coming up?

This is when you draw on the skills you've learned in training: steering, using the paddle to bypass danger, and staying upright. You remember what to do if you **capsize**. Your heart is pounding and **adrenaline** is pumping. You are ready for the challenge!

Levels of Risk

Adventure sports test your skill and knowledge against the risks of taking part. You have to make sure you are skilled enough to take on the challenge. Too little challenge might be boring. Too much could frighten you and put you at risk. The right level allows you to claim the title of Adventurer.

DID YOU KNOW?

The oldest canoe ever found is around 10,000 years old. It was **excavated** in the Netherlands. The word canoe means "dugout;" the first canoes were dug out of a tree trunk. The Inuit have used kayaks for 4,000 years. Kayak means "hunter's boat." Inuit hunters used them to catch large sea creatures—even whales.

Getting Started

Learning how to stay upright in a boat and paddle it along takes practice and patience. Start by asking for advice from experienced friends or from trainers at a canoe or kayaking club.

Where to Learn

The safest place to learn is on a slow-moving river or calm lake. You need to balance just to sit upright in a small boat, and moving the boat in a particular direction is tricky. It's best to learn with other beginners and at least one experienced paddler to help if you get into trouble.

These beginners are learning to kayak on a calm lake.

Capsizing

Before you start, make sure you can swim at least the length of a swimming pool in your clothes—that's harder than it sounds! Then start by learning what to do if you capsize so you can relax a bit, knowing you'll be able to cope with whatever happens.

What to Wear

On a warm day with warm water and nice weather, wear shorts and a T-shirt with a **life jacket** or buoyancy aid. On colder days you'll need a **thermal layer** next to the skin and a waterproof jacket with sealed cuffs and neck openings to stop water from getting in. Paddlers often wear a wetsuit. Tennis shoes are fine on your feet, although hiking sandals or water-sport shoes are better. A helmet is essential for white water to protect your face and head if you hit the boat or rocks.

Life jackets and helmets are essential safety gear for kayakers.

Amazing FACTS

The longest solo kayaking journey ever made on a river was along the mighty Amazon River in Brazil, South America. The British children's TV personality Helen Skelton paddled more than 1,860 miles (3,000 km) in 2010. She also set the record for the longest distance covered in 24 hours by a woman—75 miles (121 km)—and paddled an amazing average of 60 miles (96.5 km) a day.

Boats and Water

Boats range from a two-person slim sea kayak to the small, rounder stunt craft used in wild white water. If you plan to buy a boat, find out about the different types and talk to as many experienced people as you can first.

This is a kayak . . .

Canoe or Kayak?

A canoe and a kayak look very similar. Both are small boats in which paddlers face the way they are going (unlike rowers, which face backward). You sit inside a kayak and paddle with a double-bladed paddle. In a canoe, you either sit or kneel and paddle with a single-bladed paddle or pole.

. . . and this is a canoe.

DID YOU KNOW?

Native peoples made the first kayaks and canoes from wood bark, bone, and animal skins—even whole tree trunks sometimes.

This is a traditional Polynesian canoe.

White Water

One of the toughest places to paddle a small boat is a fast-running river. Rivers with a **gradient** big enough to allow the water to form rapids are called white water. The turning water gives kayakers and canoeists a thrilling ride. White water rivers are graded depending on how tough they are, ranging from grade 1 to grade 6. Grade 6 rivers have large rapids and big drops between hazards.

Before you set out on even a grade 1 river, you need good paddling skills, as well as a good understanding of your boat.

White-Water Grades for Rivers

Grade 1 Easy. Slow-moving water with small waves; no serious obstacles

Grade 2 Medium. Moderate rapids and other hazards

Grade 3 Difficult. High waves, larger rapids, and other hazards; check out the route first

Grade 4 Very difficult. Long rapids and high waves; dangerous hazards including rocks, strong **eddies,** and **undercurrents**; you need to be an expert with quality equipment

Grade 5 Extremely difficult. Long, violent rapids, one after the other; big drops, strong currents, and very steep gradient; extreme hazards with narrow sections

Grade 6 Very few people tackle this level. The water is so violent, and the drops so large, that there is a real danger of dying.

Boat Design

Large, stable two-person sea kayaks can travel long distances and carry heavy loads: tents, food, stoves, and more. They are easy to handle, are comfortable, and cope with sea swells. At the other extreme are stunt boats—small and unstable but easy to handle.

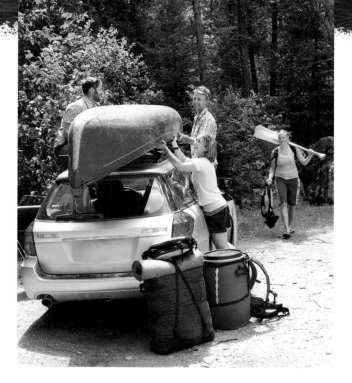

This family is loading a large canoe and supplies for a trip on the river.

Modern Kayaks

A basic modern kayak is about 13 feet (4 m) long and 2 feet (60 cm) at its widest. It is light and low in the water, with a pointed end to help carve a path. Today, most boats of this sort are made of plastic.

spraydeck

end grab

seat

back deck

cockpit

hull

end grab

front deck

paddle

Open Canoes

These boats have changed little from their original design, when they were used by native peoples to travel around waterways and carry goods. Today, canoes are still used for camping and touring trips.

stern

gunwale

yoke

paddle

seat

gunwale

seat

hull

bow

keel

TRUE Survivors

In 1793, Scottish fur trader Alexander Mackenzie crossed the Rocky Mountains in northwestern Canada to reach the Pacific Ocean in a canoe with a small team of men. He was the first to do this. He set out from Lake Athabasca in the center of Canada and covered 1,860 miles (3,000 km) of wilderness, paddling upstream as well as down and carrying his canoe between rivers. Two hundred years later, British poet and adventurer Robert Twigger made the same trip. He faced the same hazards: isolation, food shortage, attack by bears, getting lost, tackling white water rapids, and avoiding injury. His traditional birch bark canoe, stitched together with pine roots, is on display in the Peace River Town Museum in Alberta, Canada.

Danger in the Water!

Paddlers need to know the hazards they are likely to meet, whether they're paddling in a river, lake, or the sea.

overhanging branches

strainer *(fallen tree for example)*

slippery muddy bank

low bridge

strong current

weir

stopper

River Hazards

There are many natural and man-made hazards to look out for in rivers. Here are a few of the common dangers lurking in inland waterways.

rapid

waterfall

steep bank

rocks and boulders

Stoppers and Siphons

A stopper is surface water that flows backward as it goes over an object under the water. A siphon is a current of water that flows under or between obstacles, such as rocks, or disappears into a hole.

Bugs in the Water

You can catch Weil's disease from paddling in rivers and canals. It's caused by bacteria (tiny bugs) in the urine of animals such as rats and cows. If you catch it, you will have a high temperature, a bad headache, and sometimes a rash. Antibiotics cure it, but it can kill you if it's not treated.

Storms at sea are a hazard to paddlers.

Lakes and Seas

When you're paddling on a large lake or in the sea, you can lose sight of land. At sea, an offshore wind or outgoing tide can make it hard to paddle back to shore. Always carry a map and a whistle and **flares** to attract attention.

Watch the Weather

Always check the weather, especially if you are going any distance from shore. Strong wind, rain, hot sun, or a big drop in temperature can all lead to problems.

TRUE Survivors

Tyler Bradt is a 26-year-old American white water kayaker. In April 2009, he broke the world record for the longest waterfall drop—a staggering 187 feet (57 m) over the Palouse Falls in Washington. It took him four seconds in free fall to hit the water at the bottom. Bradt had trained for this feat by kayaking over bigger and bigger falls. He knew that Palouse would be more complicated than any previous waterfall. Bradt was supported by a team of nine people, including two in boats at the bottom of the fall in case he needed to be rescued. He never doubted that he could do it, even during the heart-stopping seconds when he was paddling toward the lip of the fall: "Palouse was a calculated risk, no doubt dangerous, but also one of the most amazing days of my life."

Learning to Kayak

Start from a place where it is easy to get into your boat, such as a flat water river or a lake with a bank or **jetty**. Once you are launched, stay in sight of the bank so you can get out again. Do not go alone—make sure there are two other boats with you to help if you get into trouble.

Getting into a Kayak

Draw your boat to the bank. Hold it with one hand and the bank with your other. Swing one leg into the cockpit, move forward, pull in your other leg, and sit down. Hold the bank to steady the boat, reach for your paddle, and put it across the boat so it is ready to use. Put on the spraydeck.

A paddler launches his boat from a river bank where there is flat water.

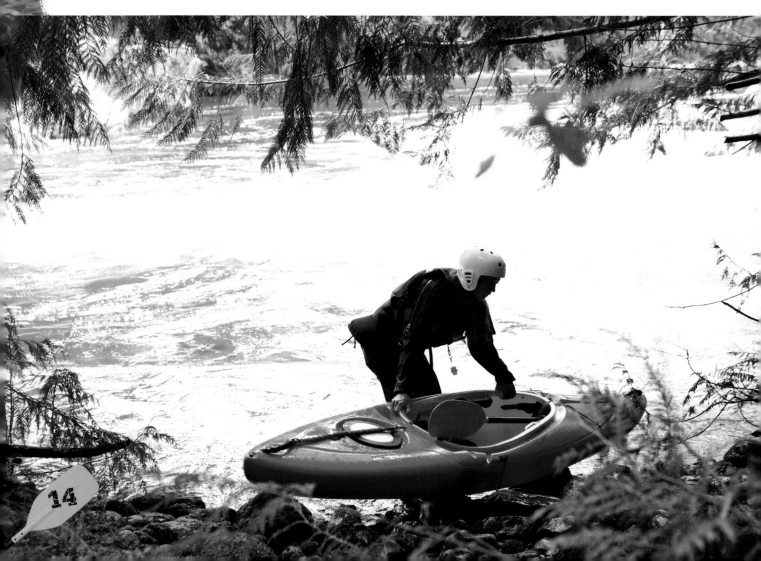

The Paddle

A kayak paddle has a **blade** at both ends. It should be the right length. If it's too long, it will be hard to handle, and if it's too short, you won't get enough power from it. When you rest one end of the paddle on the ground, the other end should be about 12 inches (30 cm) above your head.

12 in. (30 cm)

Learning how to use a double-bladed kayak paddle is a key skill.

Paddle Strokes

Forward paddle:
Reach forward, keeping the paddle close to the boat and sticking up in the air (see left). Use your body to move you forward.

Backward paddle:
Turn your shoulders, reach back with the paddle, and keep your arms as straight as possible. Try to stay in a straight line.

Stopping the Boat

When moving forward, put the blade into the water at about 90° to your boat. You should feel the pressure of the water against it. Then put the other blade into the water to slow down more and stop you from turning.

AMAZING KAYAK MARATHON

Ian Tordoff kayaked across the English Channel from Folkestone, Kent, to Wisant Beach near Calais in northern France in 3 hours and 22 minutes in May of 2005. He beat a world record that had stood for nearly 30 years. Then, in October 2007 Olympic champion Ian Wynne broke Tordoff's record by making the crossing in 2 hours, 59 minutes, and 6 seconds.

Learning to Canoe

Open canoes are great for camping trips because you can carry plenty of gear in them. Experienced paddlers can tackle quite rough water in an open canoe, but when you are learning, make sure you stay on flat water.

Getting into a Canoe

When you try to step into an open canoe, the boat will move away from the shore. Pull it to the shore and hold the near side with your paddle placed across it. Then take hold of the other side of the boat and step lightly in. Now sit or kneel.

Sit or Kneel?

Kneeling gives you better control over the boat and allows you to make stronger strokes. Keep your back straight and your knees braced against the side of the boat. Sit so your weight makes the front of the boat (the bow) rise a little out of the water. This helps you move the boat around more easily.

Paddle on both sides when trying to travel in a straight line in a large open canoe.

Paddling

A canoe paddle should come up to your chin. An open canoe paddle has one blade and is shorter than a kayak paddle. Make the strokes by putting one hand on top and the other on the **shaft**, level with the edge of the boat. Keep the paddle as close to the boat as possible. Two people can paddle together, but put the lightest person in front so the boat lifts a little.

AMAZING CANOE MARATHON

The longest nonstop, two-person canoe race in America is held every year in July. The Au Sable River International Canoe Marathon covers 120 miles (193 km), starting in Grayling and finishing in Oscoda on Lake Huron in Michigan. The race starts at 9:00 P.M. Around 100 competitors run through the streets of Grayling carrying their boats. Then they paddle through the night (between 14 and 19 hours) to reach the finish. During the race, competitors paddle at about 60 strokes a minute, making around 60,000 strokes in total. The race is one of the toughest endurance events in the world, and the winner earns prize money of more than $50,000. The fastest time for completing the race was 14 hours, 8 minutes, and 18 seconds, set by Canadian Serge Corbin and his American partner, Jeff Kolka, in 1999.

White Water

The biggest challenge for paddlers is white water. This can mean shooting the rapids on a river or taking on waves and surf at sea. Whichever form it takes, white water paddling spells excitement and danger.

Grade 5 white water presents a serious challenge for paddlers.

Never take on something you don't think you can handle. You need to know the grading system for rivers (see page 9) and learn how to look at a river and "read it." This means finding a safe route through waves, stoppers, drops, and strainers. Remember that rivers can rise or fall: heavy rain, melting snow, and hydroelectric power stations can all change a gently flowing river into a raging torrent. Storms out at sea can send a large swell toward land that whips up larger waves than usual.

Equipment

Apart from your boat and paddle (both should be quite short), you will need a helmet to protect your head from rocks, a life jacket, a **throwline**, and a knife.

Life jacket and helmet

White-Water Skills

Before taking on your first white-water river, you must have mastered all the basic paddle strokes. You need to be able to do an emergency roll and right the boat or remove the spraydeck and make a wet water exit and swim. You should also know how to help rescue a paddler in trouble. Never paddle white water alone, and make sure the distance to the next safe place to get out of the water is not too great.

Amazing FACTS

The Niagara Gorge below the Niagara Falls in Canada holds one of the hardest grade 6 rapids in the world. More than 3,300 tons (3,000 tonnes) of water sweep over the falls every minute into the raging river below. This stretch of water has a whirlpool 490 feet (150 m) deep and a section of water called the Himalayas because the standing waves are so big—up to 20 feet (6 m) high. Americans Chris Spelius and Ken Lagergren were the first to kayak down the gorge in the 1970s. The first woman to shoot these rapids was the American Carrie Ashton in the early 1980s.

Emergency on the River!

Even with the best preparation, things can go wrong. Paddlers can be injured, difficult conditions can tire you, or you might capsize and need help getting back into your boat or to the shore. You need to know what to do if any of these things happen to you or someone in your group.

Capsize Drill

💧 You must wear a life jacket. Roll over to make the kayak capsize.

💧 When upside down under water, lean forward with the paddle alongside the boat.

💧 Move the front paddle blade across the body and on to the surface of the water.

💧 At the same time, twist the upper body and hips and use the paddle to push the boat upright with you still in it.

💧 When you come to the surface, you should be leaning backward in the boat.

Knowing how to roll upright after capsizing is a key skill paddlers should learn early on.

Wet Exits

Learn how to roll or get out of a boat in calm water first before you try it on wild water. If you cannot roll, you will have to make a wet exit and swim out.

To do this in an open canoe, stay in the boat until you are completely underwater. This prevents you from being hit by the boat as it turns over. Kick with your feet and push with your hands to get away, but try to hold onto the paddle. As you come up, grab the boat too. Alternatively, jump out of the boat before it turns over. Practice both methods.

spraydeck, or spray skirt

pull tag

If your kayak has a spraydeck, grab the pull tag that releases it so you won't be trapped under the boat. Practice finding the tag with your eyes closed. Once you are free of the spraydeck, push out of the boat and swim to the surface.

Towing

Learn how to tow a boat and paddle to safety. There are several ways of doing this.

Extreme conditions require excellent skills. Make sure you are up to the challenges you take on.

21

Sea Kayaking

Imagine floating on a calm sea with the shore never far away, exploring hidden beaches and caves that few people have seen. This is the lure of sea kayaking—freedom, exploration, exercise, and fun! Before you go out, check the weather, tides, and sea. Be prepared for the worst and you will have a good time.

Safety First

Never go kayaking alone. Sea kayaks can seat one or two people, but make sure you go with at least two other boats. You never know what might happen. If the paddlers in one boat tire, the others may need to tow them to shore.

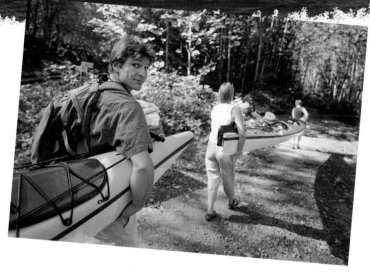

What to Take with You

Sea kayaks are longer than white water boats—13 feet (4 m) rather than 8 feet (2.5 m). They need to be stable and have storage space for extra belongings—clothes, food, water, a tent, and a stove. You also need a good map and compass and need to know how to read them.

There is safety in numbers. This group is heading off together for the coast.

Global positioning systems (**GPS**) can be very accurate and a useful backup. Other equipment should include a life jacket, a safety flare in case of an emergency, and a first aid kit.

TRUE Survivors

Aleksander Doba from Poland made the longest solo kayaking voyage ever in 2010. On October 26, Doba set off in his kayak from Dakar, Senegal, to paddle across the Atlantic Ocean to Brazil. During the trip, he encountered some tricky weather conditions, including such extreme heat that he could only paddle by night and winds that sent him around in circles. Doba eventually arrived in the mouth of the Acarau River in Brazil 99 days later and 30 lb. (14 kg) lighter, having covered 3,350 miles (5,394 km). What makes Doba's feat of strength and endurance even greater is the fact that he was 64 years old at the time. His other achievements include being the first person to circumnavigate the Baltic Sea and Baikal Lake as well as the first to paddle the entire length of the Polish coast in both directions.

Going on a Journey

Planning and going on a journey can be great fun, whether you spend just one night in a tent on the beach or take a week-long trip far from civilization.

TRUE Survivors

An inexperienced couple set off in a canoe along a 6-mile (10 km) stretch of the Snake River in Minnesota. They thought it would take about three hours to reach a place where they could get out of the river again, so they set off around midday. They took few clothes (it was warm) and only matches for emergency gear. But the river was low and sluggish, and the journey took much longer than expected. They had only traveled 3.75 miles (6 km) when the sun began to set and the temperature started to fall, making them dangerously cold.

At this point, they spotted a dim light on the riverbank. They struggled out of the water and found help in a small cabin. The couple was lucky that someone was there to help them. If you listed all the things they did wrong on this trip, the list would be quite long!

Guides and Equipment

River guide books will tell you about the **code of conduct** for the river as well as important features, white water grades, places where you can launch your boat, and places where you will need to carry the boat (called portage).

These paddlers are carrying their boat to avoid a hazard such as big rapids or waterfalls.

Before setting out on a trip, make sure that everyone is suitably equipped, and let someone know your planned route in case of emergency.

Entering Competitions

There are many types of competitions you can take part in with a kayak or canoe.

Paddlers compete in river races on flat or white water, slaloms, **freestyle races**, sprints, and marathons. You can play canoe polo or enter kayak surfing competitions.

The Olympics

Kayaks and canoes became part of the Olympic Games in 1936. Since then, the best paddlers in the world have competed at the summer games, held every four years. Olympic events include the 500 meter and 1,000 meter sprint. There can be solo paddlers or two or even four people in a boat. Heats are held with the winners going forward each time.

This man is taking part in an Olympic white water slalom competition.

TRUE SPORTSMAN

Sweden's top paddler is Anders Gustafsson, born in Jönköping in 1979. He started canoeing at age seven and was spotted by the Swedish Olympic Committee in 1999. At the time, he was in the Swedish army, working as a personal guard for the king. Gustafsson took part in his first Olympic games in Sydney in 2000 and has since become a full-time champion sprint canoeist. What makes him so good? Being 6 ft., 2 in. (1.92 m) tall helps—his long arms and legs help to power his strokes when kayaking. He trains long and hard to improve his skills and fitness.

Slalom Racing

The slalom is an exciting event held on a 980-foot (300 m) artificial white water course. Competitors paddle around a series of up to 25 gates and receive penalties if they touch them. The challenge is to master the wild water while weaving in and out of the gates, finishing in the fastest time you can. No race is more thrilling to watch than the slalom!

One of the most extreme canoe races is the Quebec ice canoe race, held every year in Canada. Teams of five compete to be the first to cross the St. Lawrence river, battling strong currents, high tides, and ice floes.

AMAZING SPRINT RECORDS

Here are some world records set by solo canoeists and kayakers in international canoe and kayaking competitions.

Men's 500 meter record: 1 minute, 34.68 seconds, set by Anders Gustafsson of Sweden in 2009.

Women's 500 meter record: 1 minute, 47.343 seconds, set by Katalin Kovacs of Hungary in 2002.

Men's 1,000 meter record: 3 minutes, 22.484 seconds, set by Max Hoff of Germany in 2011.

Women's 1,000 meter record: 3 minutes, 52.983 seconds, set by Elzbieta Urbanczik of Poland in 2001.

What do you know about paddling?

Do you think you're ready to venture onto the water? Do you know the difference between a sea kayak and a white water boat? What equipment do you need on a long journey, and how do you escape from a capsized boat? Try this quiz to find out how much you know about paddling. Answers are on page 31.

1 How many grades are there in white water paddling?
- **a** Ten
- **b** Twelve
- **c** Six
- **d** Three

2 When you capsize your boat and are underwater, what should you do?
- **a** Hold your breath and wait for rescue.
- **b** Remove any obstacles, push out of the boat, and swim to the surface.
- **c** Let go of your paddle to let people know you are in trouble.
- **d** Take off your life jacket.

1

2

3

▶3 Link these images to their names.
- **a** Weir
- **b** Stopper
- **c** Strainer
- **d** Waterfall
- **e** Rapids

4

5

◄ 4 The native peoples of the Arctic invented the kayak. True or false?

5 What is a spraydeck for?
  a Cleaning your boat
  b Keeping water out of the cockpit
  c Storing extra belongings
  d Keeping your deck of cards dry

6 What is a buoyancy aid (life jacket) for?
  a Keeping you afloat if your boat capsizes
  b Keeping your boat upright in wild water
  c Helping you get into your boat
  d Mending a hole in your boat

7 What is a siphon?
  a A small bottle for keeping your drink in
  b A small tube for getting water out of your boat
  c A place where water disappears underground and presents a hazard to paddlers
  d A sign that paddlers put on their boats

8 What is the name of the disease you can catch from paddling in some canals and rivers?
  a Influenza
  b Scarlet fever
  c Lyme disease
  d Weil's disease

9 Which of these items should you take paddling when the weather is forecasted to be cold?
  a Wetsuit or waterproof jacket
  b Thermal layer
  c Shorts
  d Sun hat

► 10 Link the following items to their names.
  a End grab
  b Hull
  c Cockpit
  d Front deck
  e Bow
  f Stern

Glossary

adrenaline A chemical our bodies make to help us run fast from danger or fight it

blade The part of a paddle that goes in the water to move the boat along

capsize To turn upside down in a boat on a river or at sea

code of conduct A set of guidelines to help people use the river responsibly and consider other users

eddies Patches of river water that flow in a circle, often beside a main current or downstream of an obstacle such as a rock

excavated Dug out of the ground

flare A device used in an emergency at sea; a flare gives off a bright light and smoke to attract attention.

freestyle races A competition held on white water; competitors perform acrobatic moves in small boats

GPS A Global Positioning System is a handheld device used to navigate where you are; it works by fixing on three or more satellites as they orbit the earth.

gradient The angle of a river bed; a steep gradient means waterfalls and rapids form; a gentle gradient means the river moves slowly.

jetty A structure that sticks out into the water from which you can launch a boat

life jacket A piece of equipment (also called a buoyancy aid) made from light material that keeps you afloat

shaft The handle of a paddle

spraydeck A tight-fitting cover that goes over you and the cockpit of your kayak; it stops water spray from getting into the boat.

strainer A hazard such as a tree with lots of branches sticking out of a river; water is "strained" through the hazard, but a boat would get trapped.

swell The rising and falling of the sea is called the swell; after a storm, there can be a very big swell.

thermal layer A layer of clothing worn next to the skin to keep you warm and dry; clothes made of wool and some artificial fibers make good thermal layers.

throwline A rope usually between 30 and 80 feet (10 and 25 m) long, used in an emergency to throw to someone in difficulty in the water

undercurrents Water under the surface that moves in a particular direction; undercurrents can be dangerous because you cannot always see them.

weir A small dam or barrier in a river that slows the flow of water; weirs can be hazardous to paddlers.

Websites

www.americancanoe.org American Canoe Association

www.canoe.org.au Australian Canoeing

www.bcu.org.uk British Canoe Union

www.irishcanoeunion.com Irish Canoe Union

www.canoenz.org.nz New Zealand Canoe Federation

Books

Canoeing and Kayaking (Get Outdoors) Lois Rock, PowerKids Press, 2010

Kayaking and Canoeing (Passport to World Sports) Paul Mason, Capstone Press, 2011

Running the Rapids: White-water Rafting, Canoeing, and Kayaking (Adrenaline Adventure) Jeff C. Young, ABDO Publishing, 2011

Quiz Answers

1 *c*

2 *b*

3 *1:d, 2:c, 3:a, 4:e, 5:b*

4 *True*

5 *b*

6 *a*

7 *c*

8 *d*

9 *a & b*

10 *1:c, 2:e, 3:d, 4:a, 5:f, 6:b.*

Index

adrenaline 5

canals 12
capsizing 5, 6, 20
challenges 4, 5, 18, 21, 27
clothing 6, 7, 23, 25
cockpits 10, 14
control 5, 16
currents 9, 12, 27

drops 9, 13, 18

eddies 9
emergencies 19, 20–21, 23, 25
end grabs 10

flares 13, 23

grades for rivers 9, 18, 19, 25
gradients 9
gunwales 11

hazards 9, 11, 12, 13, 25
helmets 7, 19
hulls 10, 11

ice 4, 27
Inuit 4, 5

keels 11

lakes 4, 6, 12, 13, 14
launching 14, 25
life jackets 7, 19, 20, 23

paddles 5, 8, 10, 11, 14, 15, 16, 19, 20, 21

racing 17, 26–27
rapids 4, 5, 9, 11, 12, 18, 19, 25
rivers 4, 5, 6, 7, 9, 10, 11, 12, 14, 18, 19, 25, 26, 27
rocks 5, 7, 9, 12, 19

safety 6, 7, 18, 19, 21, 23
sea 4, 5, 12, 13, 18, 22–23
sea kayaks 8, 10, 22–23
siphons 12
spraydecks 4, 10, 14, 19, 21
sterns 11
stoppers 12, 18
storms 13, 18
strainers 12, 18
strokes 15, 16, 17, 19, 26
stunt boats 8, 10
swells 10, 18

tides 13, 22, 27

towing 21, 23
training 5, 6, 13, 26

undercurrents 9

waterfalls 12, 13, 19, 25
waves 9, 18, 19
weather 7, 13, 18, 22, 23, 25
Weil's disease 12
weirs 12
wet exits 19, 21
whirlpools 5, 19
white water 4, 5, 7, 8, 9, 11, 13, 18–19, 25, 26
winds 13, 23